Rachel Carson

Environmentalist

by Christina Leaf

BLASTOFF!
2
READERS

BELLWETHER MEDIA • MINNEAPOLIS, MN

Note to Librarians, Teachers, and Parents:

Blastoff! Readers are carefully developed by literacy experts and combine standards-based content with developmentally appropriate text.

Level 1 provides the most support through repetition of high-frequency words, light text, predictable sentence patterns, and strong visual support.

Level 2 offers early readers a bit more challenge through varied simple sentences, increased text load, and less repetition of high-frequency words.

Level 3 advances early-fluent readers toward fluency through increased text and concept load, less reliance on visuals, longer sentences, and more literary language.

Level 4 builds reading stamina by providing more text per page, increased use of punctuation, greater variation in sentence patterns, and increasingly challenging vocabulary.

Level 5 encourages children to move from "learning to read" to "reading to learn" by providing even more text, varied writing styles, and less familiar topics.

Whichever book is right for your reader, Blastoff! Readers are the perfect books to build confidence and encourage a love of reading that will last a lifetime!

This edition first published in 2019 by Bellwether Media, Inc.

No part of this publication may be reproduced in whole or in part without written permission of the publisher. For information regarding permission, write to Bellwether Media, Inc., Attention: Permissions Department, 6012 Blue Circle Drive, Minnetonka, MN 55343.

Library of Congress Cataloging-in-Publication Data

LC record for Rachel Carson: Environmentalist available at https://lccn.loc.gov/2018033446

Text copyright © 2019 by Bellwether Media, Inc. BLASTOFF! READERS and associated logos are trademarks and/or registered trademarks of Bellwether Media, Inc. SCHOLASTIC, CHILDREN'S PRESS, and associated logos are trademarks and/or registered trademarks of Scholastic Inc., 557 Broadway, New York, NY 10012.

Editor: Kate Moening   Designer: Andrea Schneider

Printed in the United States of America, North Mankato, MN.

Table of Contents

Rachel Carson was an **environmentalist**. She was a writer and **scientist**, too.

Her book, *Silent Spring*, changed the world! It led people to care about nature.

"IN NATURE, NOTHING EXISTS ALONE." (1962)

Getting Her Start

Rachel was born in a small
Pennsylvania town in 1907.
Growing up, she loved
to explore nature.

Rachel was very shy.
She found a voice
through writing stories.

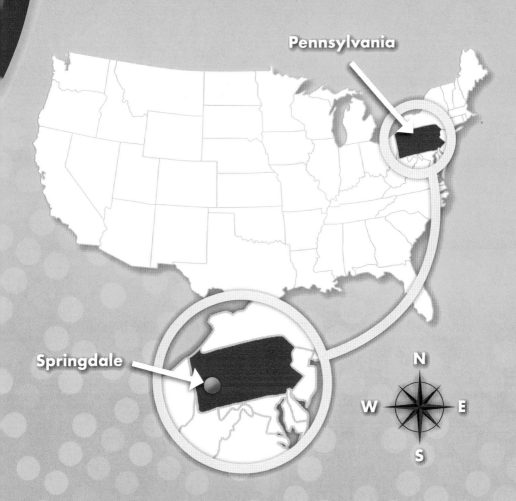

Pennsylvania

Springdale

N
W E
S

Rachel wanted to be a writer. But a teacher **inspired** her to study **biology**.

Rachel doing research off the Atlantic coast (1952)

Rachel Carson Profile

Birthday: May 27, 1907

Industry: biology

Hometown: Springdale, Pennsylvania

Education:
- biology degree
  (Pennsylvania College for Women)
- zoology degree
  (Johns Hopkins University)

Influences and Heroes:
- Maria McLean Carson (mother)
- Mary Scott Skinker (college professor)

Biology gave Rachel's writing a purpose. Oceans were her favorite subject.

Rachel became a **marine** biologist. Few women were scientists at that time.

She also wrote about science for newspapers and the radio.

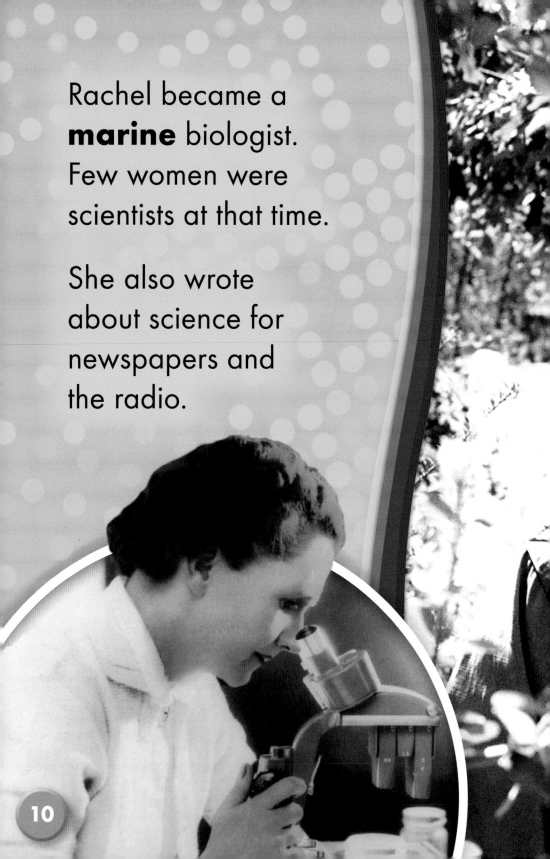

"THE HISTORY OF LIFE ON EARTH HAS BEEN A HISTORY OF **INTERACTION BETWEEN LIVING THINGS AND THEIR SURROUNDINGS.**" (1962)

Rachel receiving the National Book Award (1952)

Rachel began to **publish** books based on her scientific work. Her books won **awards**!

Her writing made it easy to understand tough scientific **topics**.

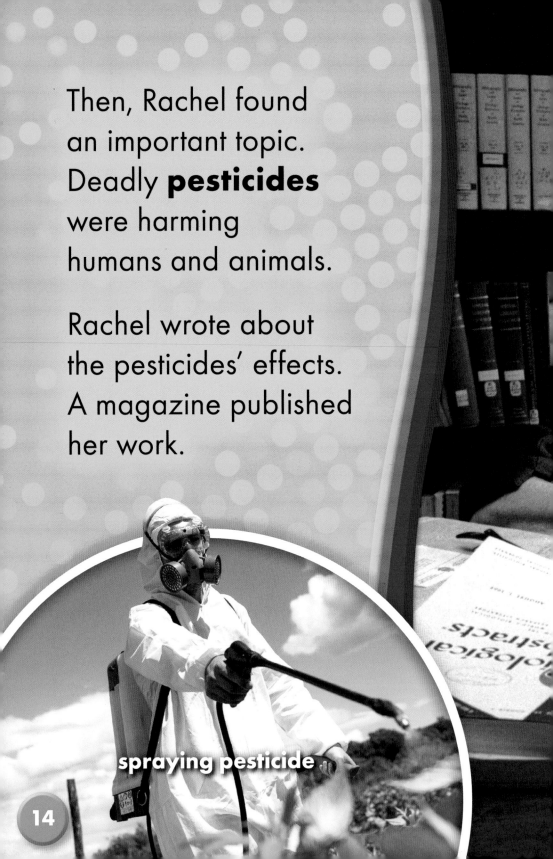

Then, Rachel found an important topic. Deadly **pesticides** were harming humans and animals.

Rachel wrote about the pesticides' effects. A magazine published her work.

spraying pesticide

Rachel's writings became a book called *Silent Spring*.

Rachel speaking to the government about pesticides (1963)

Businesses fought against Rachel. They said her **research** was wrong. But readers trusted Rachel.

Rachel's Legacy

spraying a farm
for pests

Rachel passed away soon after
Silent Spring was published.
But change had already begun.

Rachel Carson Timeline

1907	Rachel is born in Springdale, Pennsylvania
1941	*Under the Sea-Wind*, Rachel's first book, is published
1962	*Silent Spring* is published
1964	Rachel passes away in Silver Spring, Maryland

People were angry about the danger of **chemicals**.

Silent Spring's effects spread far. Certain pesticides were banned. The government began to **protect** the environment and animals.

Rachel's work made the world a safer place!

photo from the air of the Rachel Carson National Wildlife Refuge

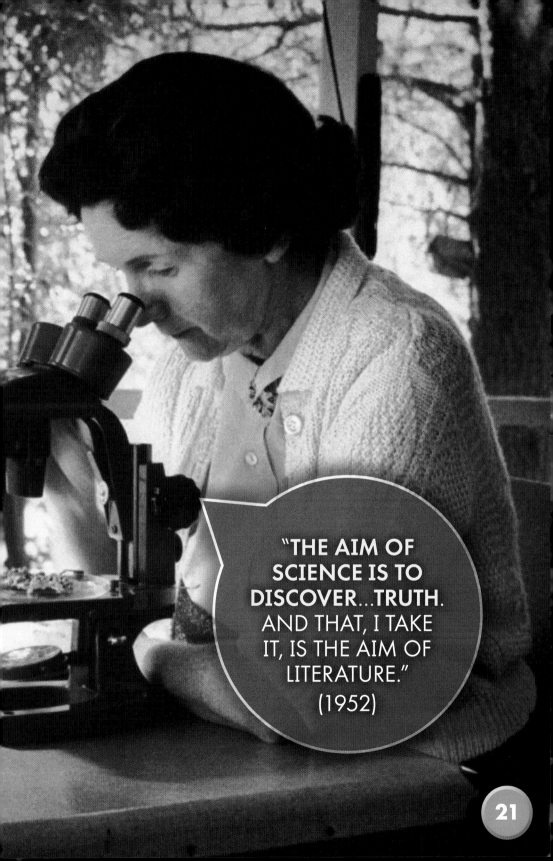

"THE AIM OF SCIENCE IS TO DISCOVER...TRUTH. AND THAT, I TAKE IT, IS THE AIM OF LITERATURE." (1952)

Glossary

awards—rewards or prizes that are given for a job well done

biology—the scientific study of life

chemicals—materials that can cause a change

environmentalist—a person who cares about the natural world

inspired—gave someone an idea about what to do or create

marine—related to the sea; marine biology is the study of life in oceans.

pesticides—materials that kill pests such as insects or weeds

protect—to keep safe

publish—to print for a public audience

research—the information collected on a subject

scientist—a person who is trained in science and whose job involves doing research or solving scientific problems

topics—subjects someone talks or writes about

To Learn More

AT THE LIBRARY

James, Emily. *Rachel Carson*. North Mankato, Minn.:
Capstone Press, 2017.

Simons, Lisa M. Bolt. *Rachel Carson: a 4D Book*.
North Mankato, Minn.: Capstone Press, 2019.

Sisson, Stephanie Roth. *Spring After Spring: How
Rachel Carson Inspired the Environmental Movement*.
New York, N.Y.: Roaring Brook Press, 2018.

ON THE WEB

FACTSURFER

Factsurfer.com gives you
a safe, fun way to find
more information.

1. Go to www.factsurfer.com.

2. Enter "Rachel Carson" into the search box.

3. Click the "Surf" button and select your
   book cover to see a list of related web sites.

Index

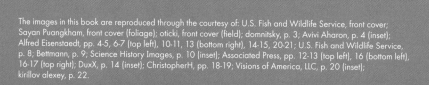